our very special
teacher, with
your first class.
1971-1973

MY SWEET LORD

MY SWEET LORD

SELECTIONS FROM
GOOD NEWS FOR MODERN MAN,
THE NEW ENGLISH VERSION
OF THE NEW TESTAMENT

illustrated by
NORMAN LALIBERTE

edited by
LOIS HUFFMON

HALLMARK EDITIONS

Copyright © 1972 by Hallmark Cards, Inc., Kansas City, Missouri. All Rights Reserved. Printed in the United States of America. Library of Congress Catalog Card Number: 73-168972. Standard Book Number: 87529-239-9.

From the Today's English Version of the New Testament. Copyright © American Bible Society 1966.

MY SWEET LORD

RIGHTEOUSNESS IS THE HARVEST THAT is PRODUCED FROM THE SEEDS

THE PEACEMAKERS PLANTED in PEACE.

JAMES 3:18

I MAY HAVE THE GIFT OF INSPIRED PREACHING; I MAY HAVE ALL KNOWLEDGE & UNDERSTAND ALL SECRETS; I MAY HAVE ALL THE FAITH NEEDED TO MOVE MOUNTAINS -- BUT IF I HAVE NOT LOVE, I AM NOTHING.

1 CORINTHIANS 13:2

HAPPY ARE THOSE WHO WORK FOR PEACE AMONG MEN: GOD WILL CALL THEM HIS SONS!

MATTHEW 5:9

LET US NOT BECOME TIRED OF DOING GOOD; FOR IF WE DO NOT GIVE UP,

THE TIME WILL COME WHEN WE WILL REAP THE HARVEST.

GALATIANS 6:9

Love is patient & kind; love is not jealous, or conceited, or proud; love is not ill-mannered, or selfish, or irritable. Love does not keep a record of wrongs; love is not happy with evil, but is happy with the truth. Love never gives up: its faith, hope, & patience never fail. 1 CORINTHIANS 13:4, 5, 6, 7

A GOOD MAN BRINGS GOOD OUT OF THE TREASURE OF GOOD THINGS IN HIS HEART; A BAD MAN BRINGS BAD OUT OF HIS TREASURE OF BAD THINGS.

FOR A MAN'S MOUTH SPEAKS WHAT HIS HEART IS FULL OF.

LUKE 6:45

OUR LOVE SHOULD NOT BE JUST WORDS & TALK; IT MUST BE TRUE LOVE,

WHICH SHOWS ITSELF IN ACTION.

1 JOHN 3:18

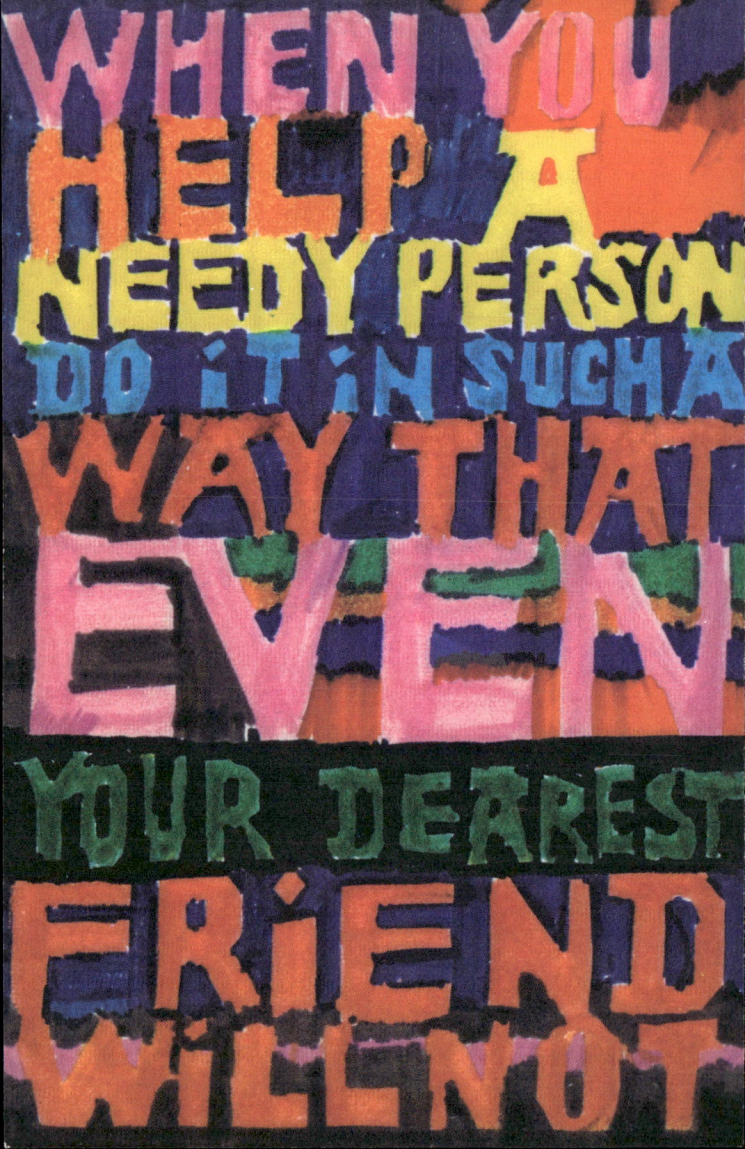

DO NOT WORRY ABOUT TOMORROW;

IT WILL HAVE ENOUGH WORRIES OF ITS OWN.

THERE IS NO NEED TO ADD TO THE TROUBLES EACH DAY BRINGS.

MATTHEW 6:25

TO HAVE FAITH IS TO BE SURE OF THINGS WE HOPE FOR,

TO BE CERTAIN OF THE THINGS WE CANNOT SEE. HEBREWS 11:1

ASK, & YOU WILL RECEIVE; SEEK, & YOU WILL FIND; KNOCK, & THE DOOR WILL BE OPENED TO YOU.

MATTHEW 7:7

GOD TREATS ALL MEN ALIKE. WHOEVER FEARS HIM & DOES WHAT IS RIGHT IS ACCEPTABLE TO HIM NO MATTER WHAT RACE HE BELONGS TO.

ACTS 10:34, 35

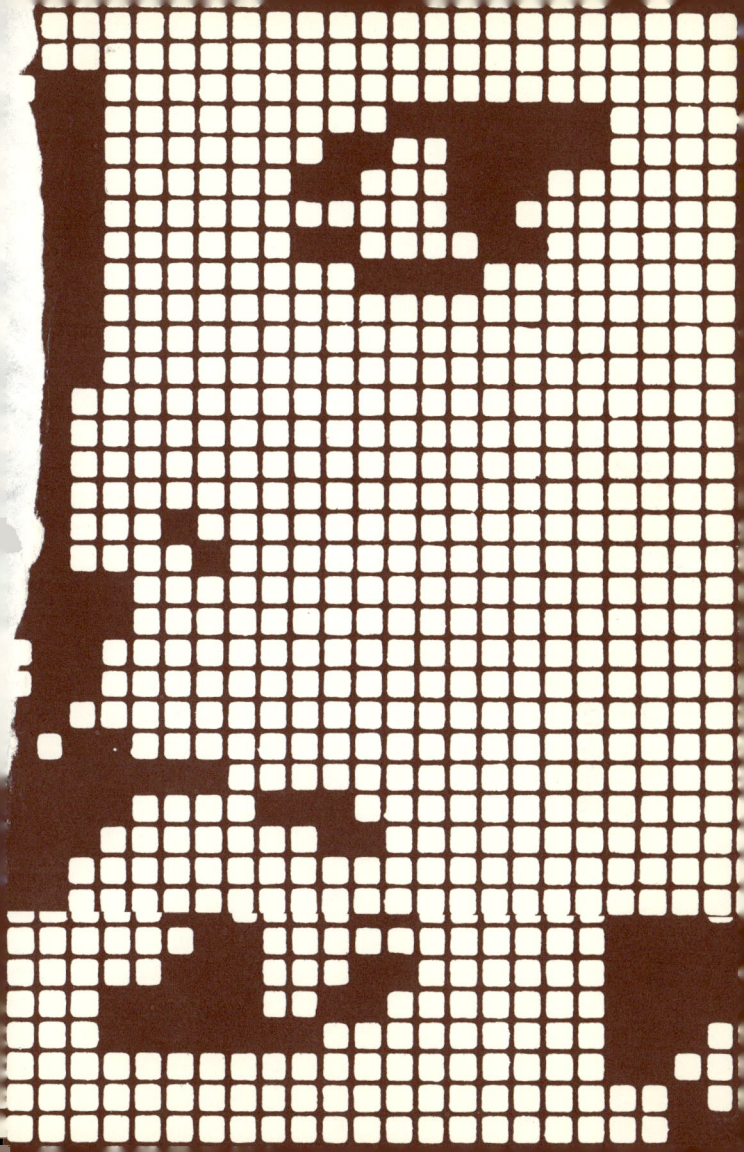

YOU
SHOULD HAVE
IS TO
LOVE
ONE ANOTHER...

ROMANS 13:8

STOP JUDGING
BY EXTERNAL
STANDARDS,

ANY COUNTRY THAT DIVIDES ITSELF INTO GROUPS THAT FIGHT EACH OTHER WILL NOT LAST VERY LONG. & ANY TOWN

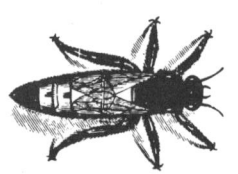

OR FAMILY THAT DIVIDES ITSELF INTO GROUPS THAT FIGHT EACH OTHER WILL FALL APART.

MATTHEW 12:25

DO NOT LET ANYONE LOOK DOWN ON YOU BECAUSE YOU ARE YOUNG, BUT BE AN EXAMPLE FOR THE BELIEVERS, IN YOUR SPEECH, YOUR CONDUCT, YOUR LOVE, FAITH, & PURITY.

1 TIMOTHY 4:12

LOVE MUST BE COMPLETELY SINCERE. HATE WHAT IS EVIL, HOLD ON TO WHAT IS GOOD. LOVE ONE ANOTHER WARMLY AS BROTHERS IN CHRIST, AND BE EAGER TO SHOW RESPECT FOR ONE ANOTHER.

ROMANS 12:9, 10

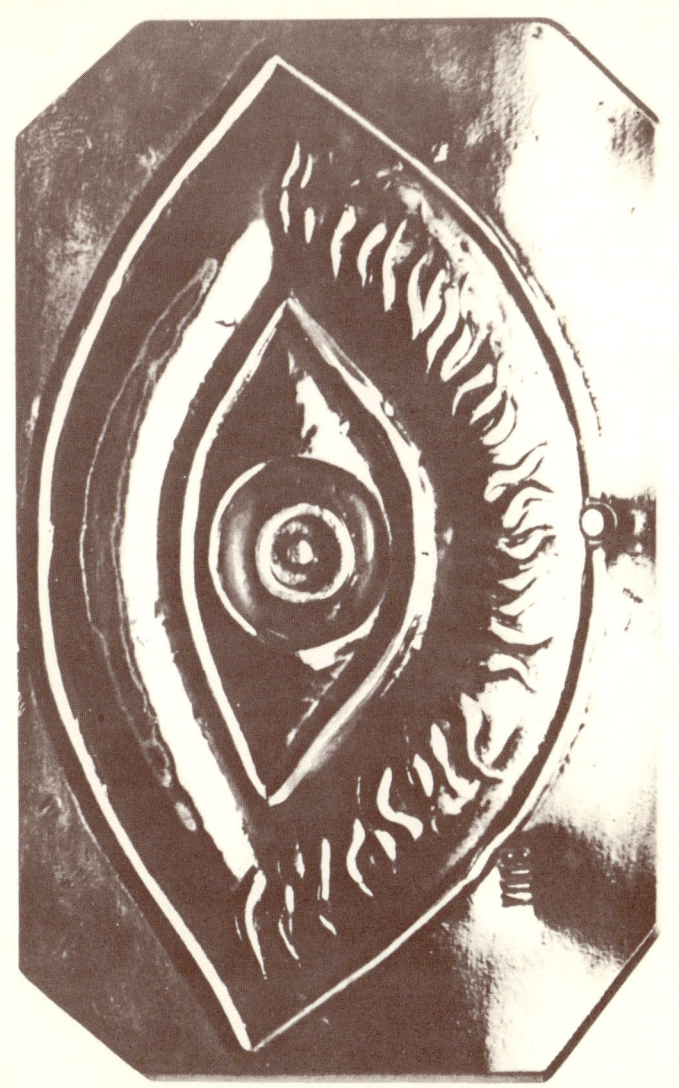

REMEMBER, I WILL BE WITH YOU ALWAYS, TO THE END OF THE AGE.

MATTHEW 28:20